THE AIR ABOVE JAMAICA BAY

THE AIR ABOVE JAMAICA BAY

STRUCTURES OF COASTAL RESILIENCE

Jamaica Bay Team
Spitzer School of Architecture
The City College of New York

Catherine Seavitt Nordenson, editor
Associate Professor of Landscape Architecture

Kjirsten Alexander
Research Associate

Danae Alessi
Research Associate

Eli Sands
Research Assistant

JAMAICA BAY PAMPHLET LIBRARY
09 The Air Above Jamaica Bay

ISBN 978-1-942900-09-2

CONTACT
Catherine Seavitt Nordenson
cseavittnordenson@ccny.cuny.edu
www.structuresofcoastalresilience.org

SCR Jamaica Bay Team
The City College of New York
Spitzer School of Architecture
Program in Landscape Architecture, Room 2M24A
141 Convent Avenue New York, New York 10031

COVER
Ring-billed gull, number culled.

supported by

THE ROCKEFELLER FOUNDATION

SCR
Structures of Coastal Resilience

CUNY
The City University of New York

The City College of New York

Oystercatchers, marsh and Manhattan skyline.   photo: Don Riepe

JoCo Marsh and JFK Airport Runway. image: Google Earth

In early 2014, after months of strident protests from the Audubon Society and other environmental activists, the Port Authority of New York and New Jersey released a statement agreeing to cease the culling of snowy owls that cross over New York's John F. Kennedy and LaGuardia Airport runways. Instead, the Port Authority will implement a "trap and relocate" management plan for snowy owls, which have recently appeared in the New York area in increasing numbers. This is an important step towards a more humane way of reducing the risk of aircraft bird strikes and protecting air travelers. However, many less charismatic birds that unknowingly trespass into JFK or LaGuardia's airspace are not given the same consideration.

Barn swallow

14

American Oystercatcher

6

American Black Duck

20

Double-crested Cormorant

270

Mute Swan

14

Killdeer

42

Mourning Dove

1,124

Fish Crow

43

Atlantic Brant

521

Ring-billed Gull

277

American Crow

8

Greater Black-backed Gull

281

Rock Dove

172

Brown-headed Cowbird

467

Laughing Gull

4,127

European Starling

909

11
Osprey

55
Mallard

1,337
Herring Gull

131
Canada goose

After the retreat of the Wisconsin Glaciation, over 40,000 years ago, wetland marshes formed in this protected estuarine embayment at the outwash plain of the terminal moraine ridge that crosses Long Island. Since then, hundreds of bird species have relied on Jamaica Bay for habitat and sustenance. The Jamaica Bay Wildlife Refuge was created by Robert Moses in 1951, and was later incorporated into the larger Gateway National Recreation Area in 1974, when the Bay was officially established as part of the National Parks System. New York City Audubon recently reported that over sixty species found at the Jamaica Bay Wildlife Refuge are on the New York State list of "Species with Significant Conservation Need."

1
American Kestrel

NPS ranger. photo: Don Riepe

JFK AIRPORT

Least tern
Common tern
Common tern
Least tern
Common tern
Common tern
Common tern
Least tern
Common tern
Common tern
Common tern
Least tern
Common tern
Seabeach amaranth
Piping plover
Black skimmer
Piping plover
Seabeach amaranth
Piping plover
Least tern
Common tern
Piping plover
Piping plover
Least tern

Peregrine falcon

Common tern
Least tern
Common loon
Piping plover
Piping plover

Common tern
Least tern   Roseate tern
Black skimmer
Piping plover

DREDGED AREAS

Threatened / Endangered Species Area

Threatened Plant

Present in Jamaica Bay

Black rail

Leatherback sea turtle

Loggerhead sea turtle

EXISTING SALT MARSH

NEW YORK CITY
DEPARTMENT OF PARKS AND RECREATION

NATIONAL PARK SERVICE
GATEWAY NATIONAL RECREATION AREA

ENVIRONMENTAL SENSITIVITY INDEX MAP
data source: NOAA

Species	State /Federal	Threatened/ Endangered	Jan Feb Mar Apr May Jun Jul Aug Sep Oct Nov Dec	Notes
Black rail	S	E		Present in Jamaica bay and marshes
Black skimmer	S	S		Nesting: May-Sept; present near Breezy Point ocean front and Atlantic Beach near western tip
Common loon	S	S		Present in Atlantic Ocean
Common tern	S	T		Nesting: May-Sept; present near Breezy Point ocean front and NW near Rockaway Inlet, Little Egg, Yellow Bar, JoCo marsh, SE portion of Rockaway Community Park, JFK (SE), Inwood (NW), and Atlantic Beach near western tip
Least tern	S	T		Present near Breezy Point ocean front (nesting May-Sept) and NW near Rockaway Inlet, SE portion of Rockaway Community Park, JKF (SE), Averne, Inwood (NW) and Atlantic Beach near western tip
Peregrine falcon	S	E		Nesting: May-Sept; present at Marine Parkway Gil Hodges Memorial Bridge
Piping plover	S/F	E/T		Nesting: April-Aug; present near Breezy Point ocean front and NW tip near Rockaway Inlet, Jacob Riis ocean front, Arverne ocean front, Edgemere ocean front and Atlantic Beach near western tip
Roseate tern	S/F	E/E		Nesting: May-Aug; present near Breezy Point ocean front
Shortnose Sturgeon	S/F	E/E		Juveniles/Adults: Jan-Dec; present in Raritan Bay
Fin whale	S/F	E/E		Present in Atlantic Ocean in NY State waters, East River and Atlantic Ocean NJ State waters (April, Sept-Nov)
Humpback whale	S/F	E/E		Present in Atlantic Ocean in NY State waters, East River and Atlantic Ocean NJ State waters (April, Sept-Nov)
Northern right whale	S/F	E/E		Present in Atlantic Ocean in NJ State waters
Leatherback sea turtle	S/F	E/E		Present in Jamaica Bay, Atlantic Ocean (including NY/NJ State waters), Raritan Bay and East River (July-Sept)
Loggerhead sea turtle	S/F	T/T		Present in Jamaica Bay, Atlantic Ocean (including NY/NJ State waters), Raritan Bay and East River (July-Sept)

Plane over West Pond, 1985.   photo: Don Riepe

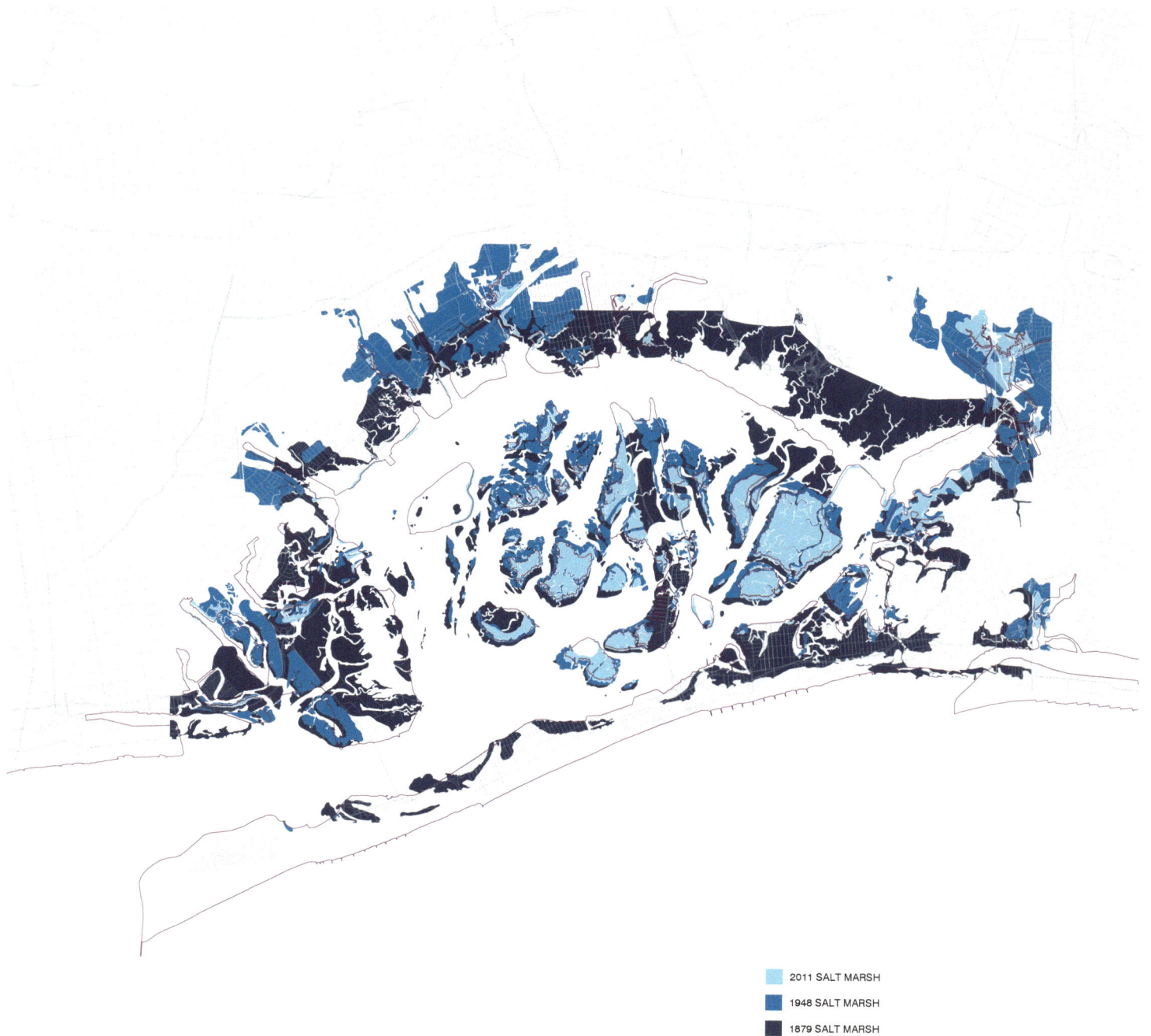

▢	2011 SALT MARSH
▢	1948 SALT MARSH
▢	1879 SALT MARSH

SALT MARSH LOSS AT JAMAICA BAY, 1879-2011
data source: NOAA

JAMAICA BAY

Increasing urbanization and marsh loss due to fill, pollution, and sea level rise along the entire eastern seaboard has reduced the available resources for birds along the Atlantic migratory flyway. Jamaica Bay has become an even more vital resource for these birds, a site to rest and store enough energy to complete their journeys north or south each season.

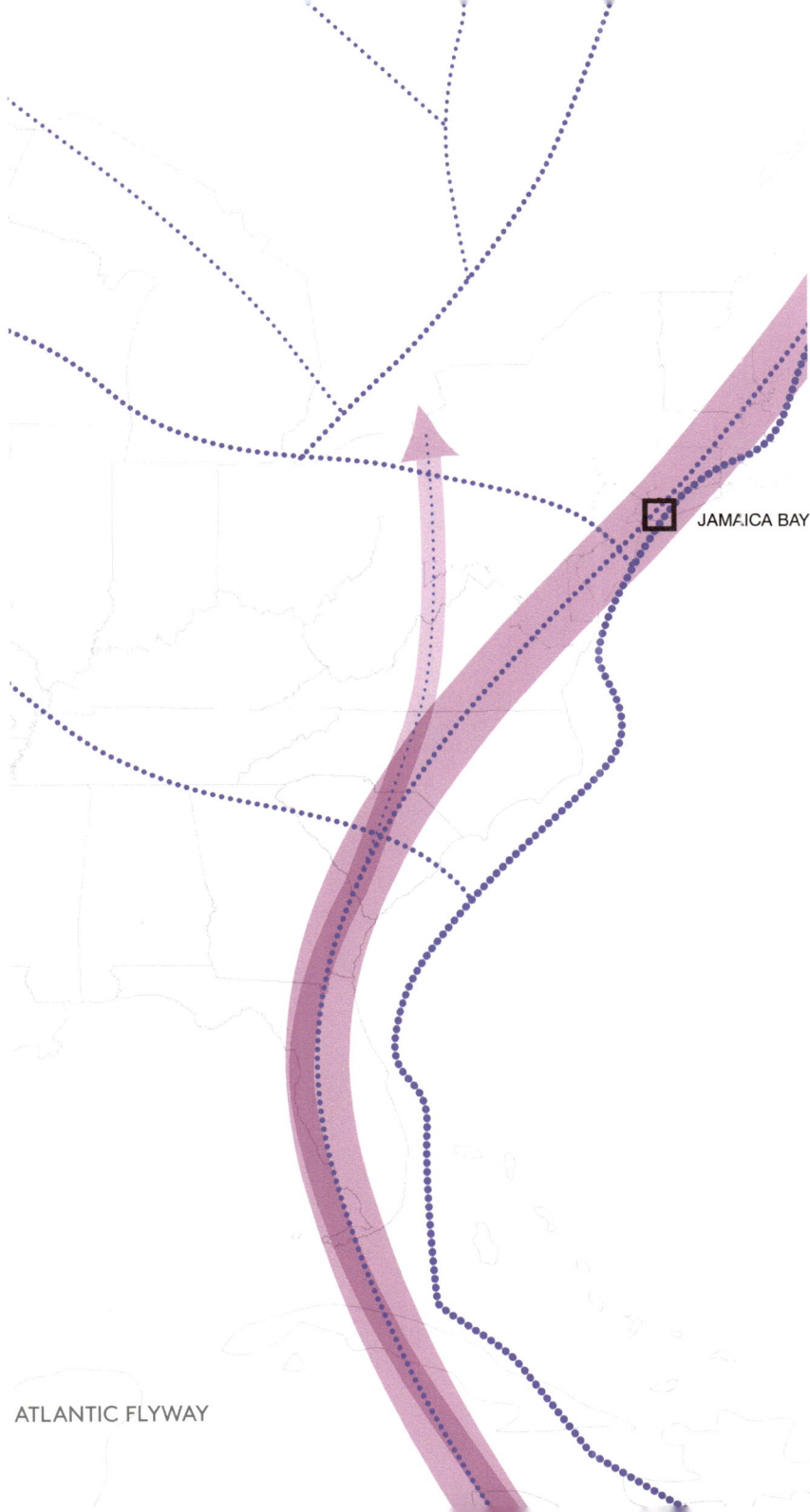

ATLANTIC FLYWAY

In 1948, Idlewild Airport opened at the eastern edge of Jamaica Bay, Queens. Its runways and terminals were constructed on filled marshlands. Renamed John F. Kennedy International Airport in 1963, it is one of the busiest international airports in the United States. On average, over one thousand flights take off and land each day from its runways. Since the establishment of the airport, bird species and aircraft have had competing demands for both ground and air space. The airport has been upgraded multiple times to accommodate larger aircraft; in the mid-1960s a major runway was extended south-west into JoCo Marsh, the largest and most intact salt marsh island in Jamaica Bay.

Cormorants, JoCo Marsh and JFK Airport, 1988.   photo: Don Riepe

JoCo Marsh and JFK Airport.   photo: Catherine Seavitt

RELATIVE AREA IN PLAN: % OF TIDAL ZONE		
6%	46%	48%

MHHW — 7.74
MHW — 7.41 — HIGH MARSH

LOW MARSH

NAVD88 — 5.33 — TOPO ZERO
MSL — 5.09
MTL — 5.06

MUD FLAT

-2.82

MLW — 2.71
MLLW — 2.51 — NOAA DEPTHS

STATION DATUM — 0.00

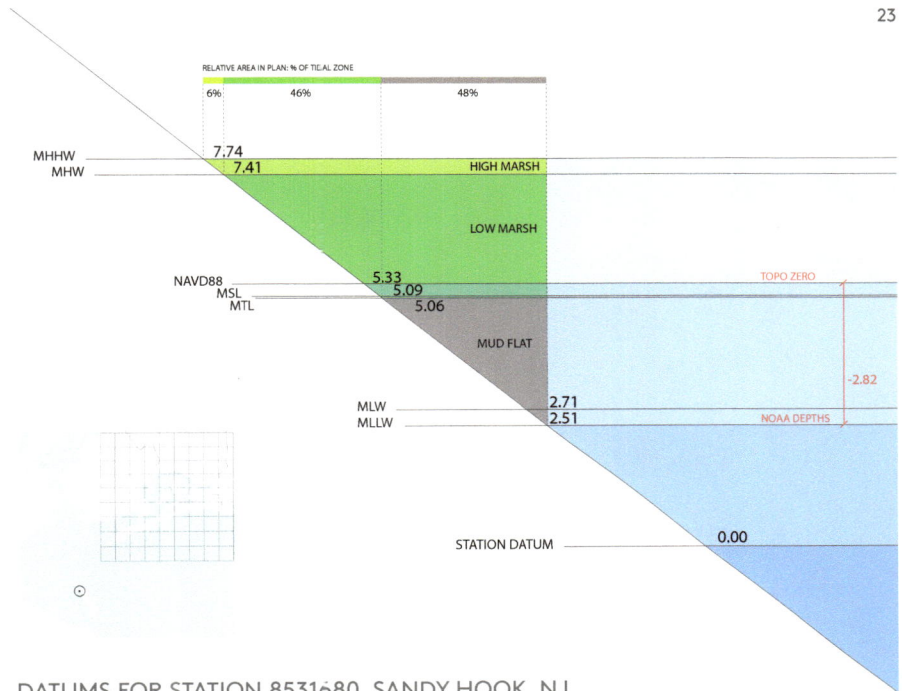

DATUMS FOR STATION 8531680 SANDY HOOK, NJ

JFK Airport and the Gateway National Recreation Area are in the same place for similar reasons: both airplane runways and marshlands require topography that is essentially flat. Large areas with little elevation change allow broad swaths of *Spartina alterniflora* marsh grasses to exist within the sensitive tidal range of mean tide to high tide. Economics and land value also played an important role in the adjacent siting of these seemingly incompatible land uses. At the time of the airport's establishment, the wetlands within and surrounding Jamaica Bay were not considered desirable enough to develop as densely as other parts of New York City, nor were they considered ecologically valuable enough to protect from development. There was room for the vast stretches of pavement that airplanes demand, and little environmental regulation in place to prevent the dredging of Grassy Bay to fill the adjacent marshland, creating solid ground for the airport.

BOROUGH OF BROOKLYN

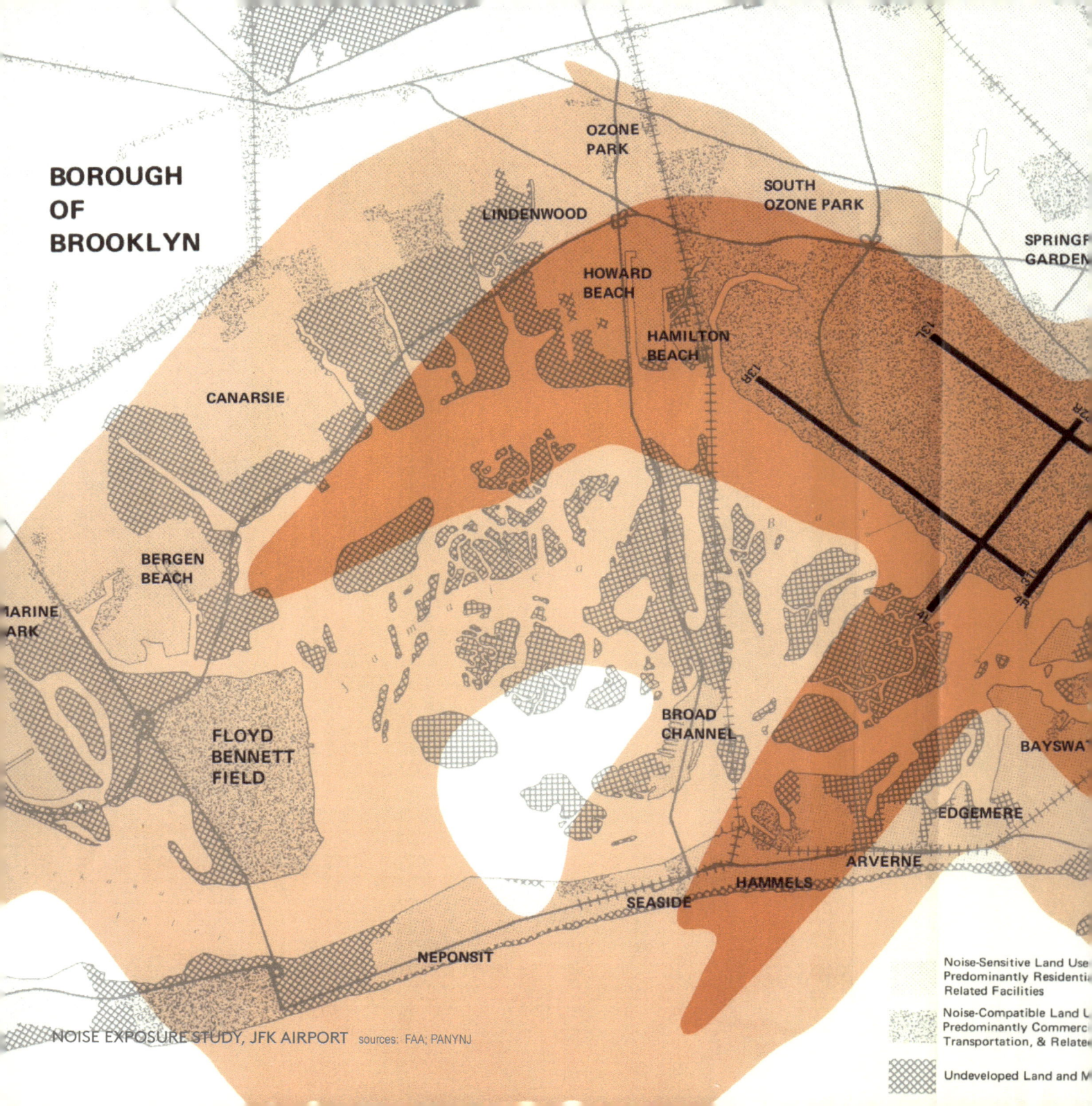

OZONE PARK

LINDENWOOD

SOUTH OZONE PARK

SPRINGF
GARDE

HOWARD BEACH

HAMILTON BEACH

CANARSIE

13R

13L

31R

BERGEN BEACH

MARINE ARK

4L

4R

FLOYD BENNETT FIELD

Jamaica *Bay*

BROAD CHANNEL

BAYSWA

EDGEMERE

ARVERNE

HAMMELS

SEASIDE

NEPONSIT

NOISE EXPOSURE STUDY, JFK AIRPORT   sources: FAA; PANYNJ

Noise-Sensitive Land Use
Predominantly Residentia
Related Facilities

Noise-Compatible Land U
Predominantly Commerc
Transportation, & Relate

Undeveloped Land and M

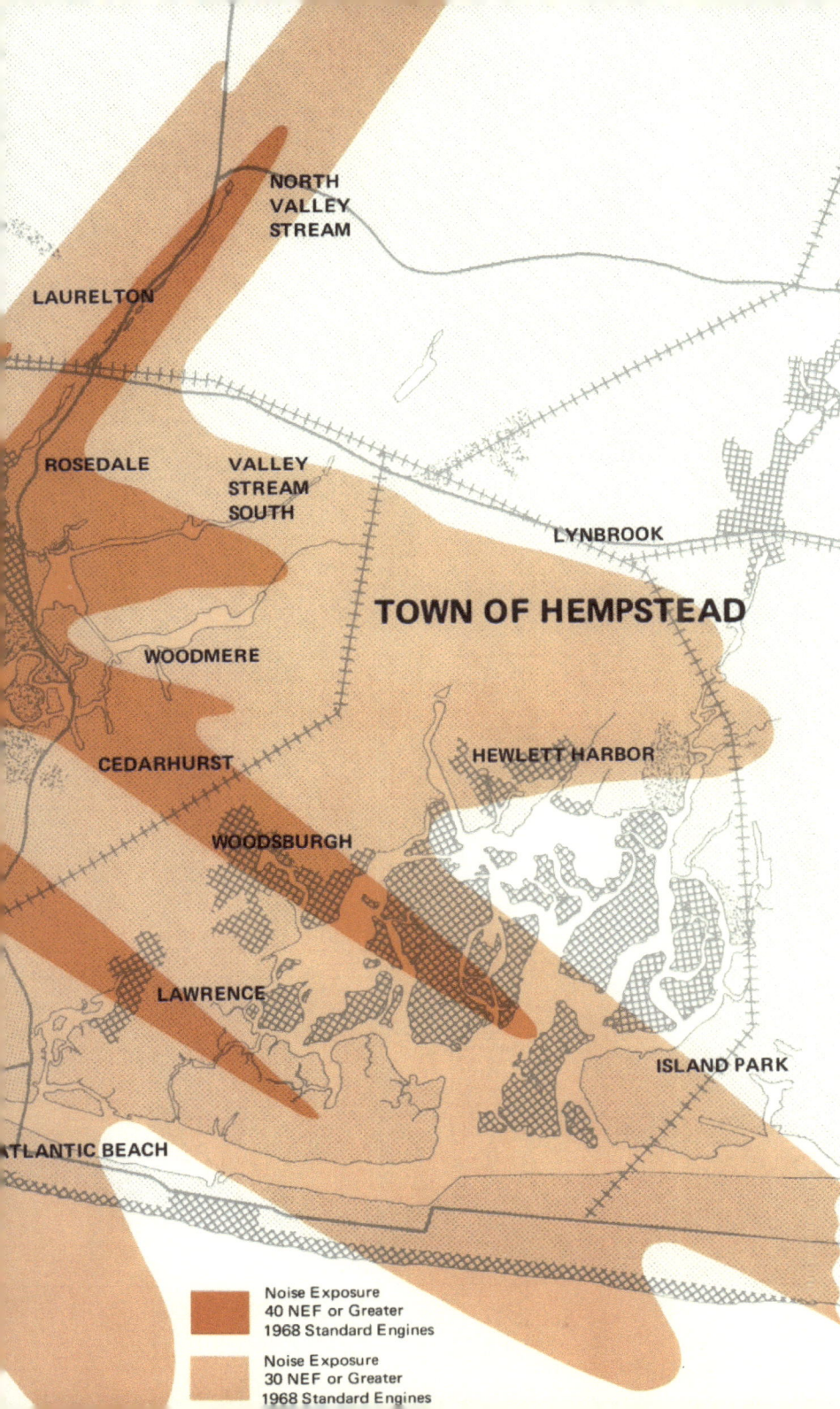

NORTH
VALLEY
STREAM

LAURELTON

ROSEDALE

VALLEY
STREAM
SOUTH

LYNBROOK

TOWN OF HEMPSTEAD

WOODMERE

HEWLETT HARBOR

CEDARHURST

WOODSBURGH

LAWRENCE

ISLAND PARK

ATLANTIC BEACH

Noise Exposure
40 NEF or Greater
1968 Standard Engines

Noise Exposure
30 NEF or Greater
1968 Standard Engines

In addition to tension on the ground between marshland and pavement, avian and aircraft interests compete in the skies. Complex flight maps reveal the highly controlled airspace surrounding the New York metropolitan region. Vital radial and sectional lines divide the airspace into safe corridors for flying craft. Although these invisible highways shift to align with wind and weather, they follow logical patterns and are very precise. Safety is paramount in air travel, and these boundaries are strictly controlled. The birds, however, are oblivious.

Laughing Gull high marsh nesting area, JoCo Marsh, c. 1990   photo: Don Riepe

The Port Authority has complete control over the airspace it manages, and concerns over aircraft bird strikes trump the complex needs of wildlife and habitat. Given its adjacency to an avian oasis, JFK Airport has developed many strategies to clear birds from its airspace. Employees shoot flares to scare birds away, post signs in cab driver break areas to discourage feeding the birds, and, most controversially, cull the most threatening species by poisoning, live trapping, sniper shooting, and euthanasia. An unofficial agreement exists among stakeholders that no high marsh will be restored east of the Cross Bay Boulevard, the causeway that transverses the Bay from north to south and divides it approximately in half. High marsh has a much narrower elevational range and a more diverse vegetation spectrum than low marsh, making it both less common and more ecologically valuable and attractive to birds. New York City Audubon has identified high salt marsh as the most crucial habitat for bird species.

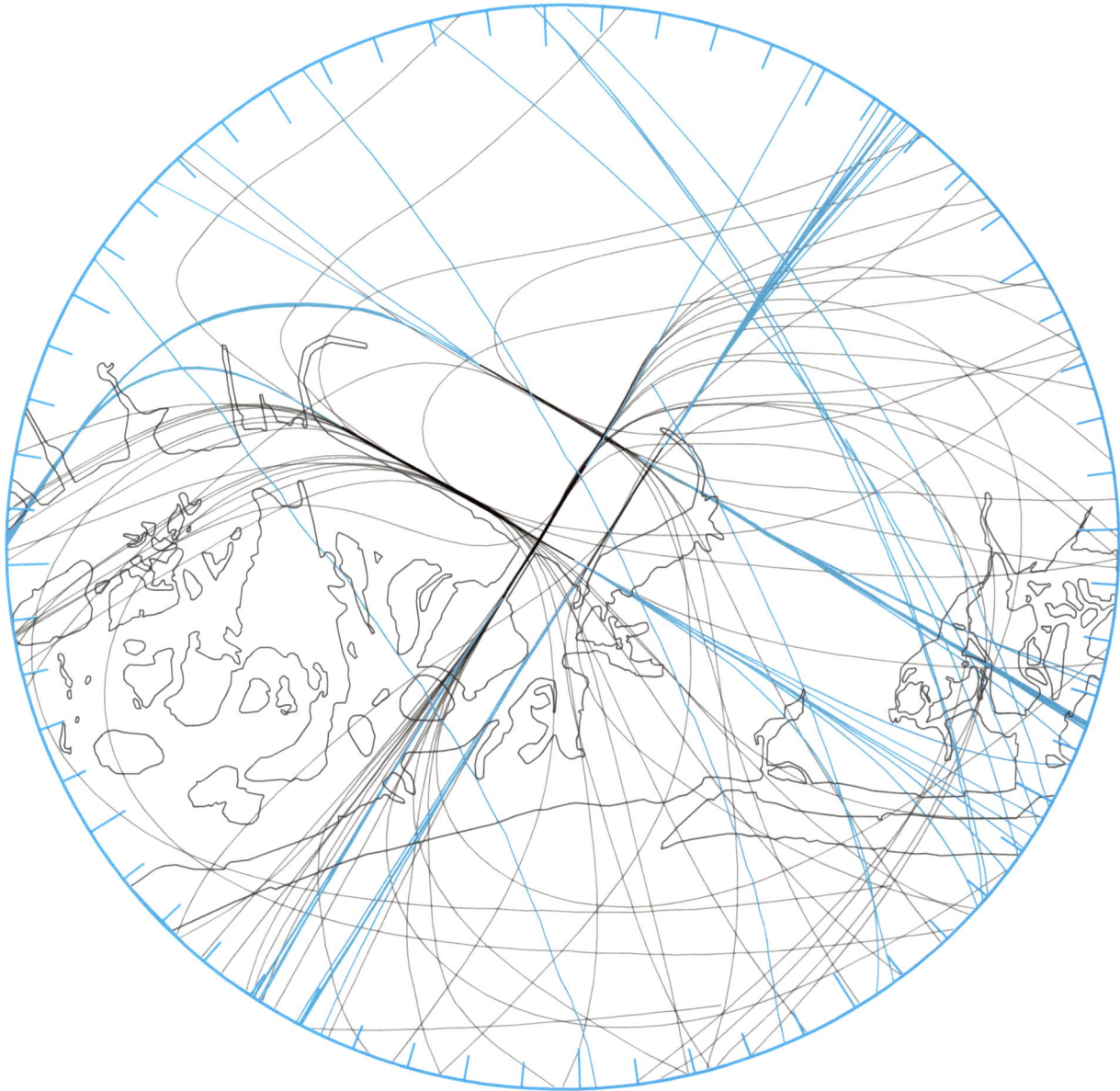

JFK GENERALIZED FLIGHT TRACKS
—— Arrival Flight Tracks
—— Departure Flight Tracks
sources: FAA; Landrum and Brown

7100'
7000'
6900'
6800'
6700'
6600'
6500'
6400'
6300'
6200'
6100'
6000'
5900'
5800'
5700'
5600'
5500'
5400'
5300'
5200'
5100'
5000'
4900'
4800'
4700'
4600'
4500'
4400'
4300'
4200'
4100'
4000'
3900'
3800'
3700'
3600'
3500'
3400'
3300'
3200'
3100'
3000'
2900'
2800'
2700'
2600'
2500'
2400'
2300'
2200'
2100'
2000'
1900'
1800'
1700'
1600'
1500'
1400'
1300'
1200'
1100'
1000'
900'
800'
700'
600'
500'
400'
300'
200'
100'
SFC

70 +12

70 SFC

70 SFC

70 15

70 +05

A

FAA CLASS B AIRSPACE

Section A

7000'

1500'

500'
SFC

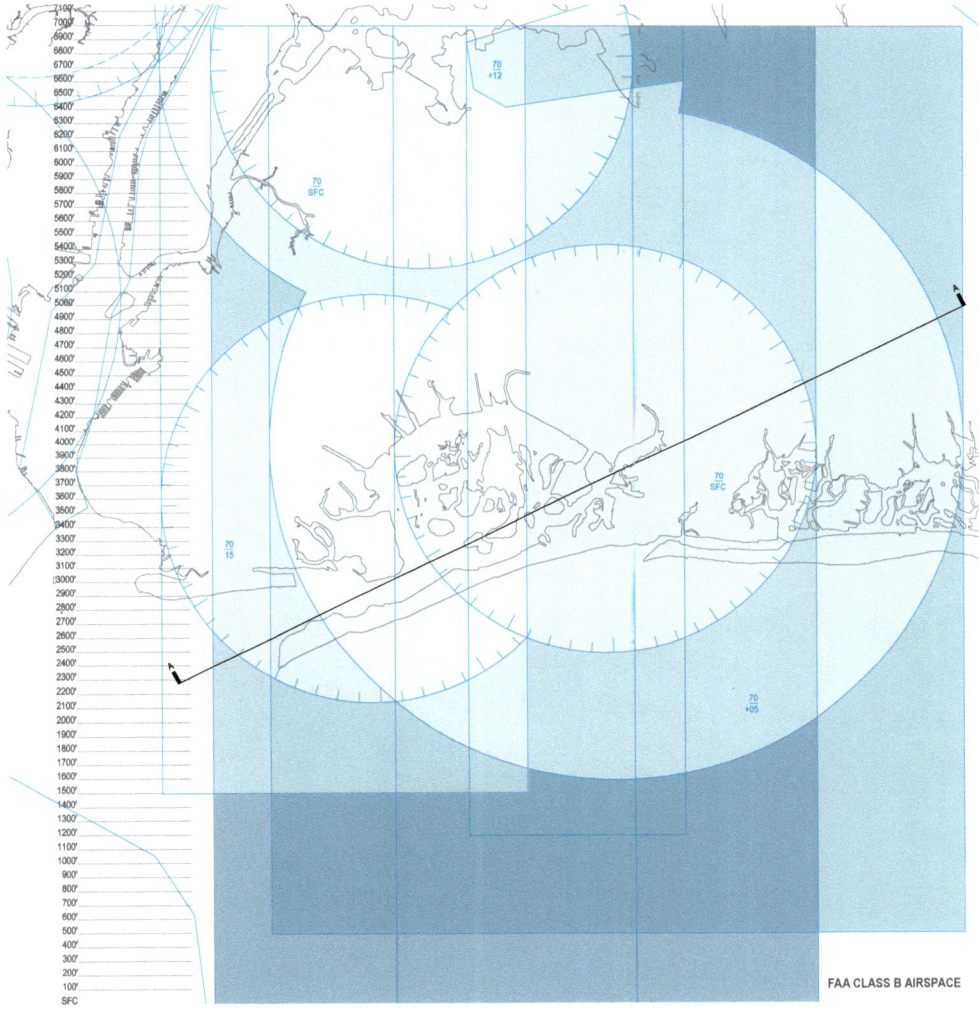

PLAN AND SECTION OF FAA-REGULATED AIRSPACE AT JAMAICA BAY
sources: FAA; PANYNJ

JFK Airport Runway 4L / 22R.   photo: Don Riepe

Snowy Owl at Jamaica Bay.   photo: Don Riepe

Public outcry has proven that the general public is uncomfortable with the idea of killing birds that are innocently in the way, particularly birds that have found sanctuary in an official refuge. The Port Authority couches its culling practices in veiled language, discussing the number of birds "taken," and bird control through "depredation" (a term defined by Merriam Webster as to plunder, lay waste, ravage). The Port Authority's recent show of support for the trapping and relocation of snowy owls is a hopeful signal for more flexible mediation in the future. The level of success for this initiative remains to be seen, however, as relocated birds often return after being released elsewhere, and as local populations of common species such as the laughing gull and the Canada goose expand, the relocation of each offending bird is unlikely. The dynamics of this shared space will continue to be complex.

Nesting area on Canarsie Pol. photo: Don Riepe

JFK Runway and JoCo Marsh.   photo: Don Riepe

www.ingramcontent.com/pod-product-compliance
Lightning Source LLC
Chambersburg PA
CBHW060826270326
41931CB00002B/81